My Home Scavenger Hunt

Bela Davis

T0021062

Abdo Kids Junior
is an Imprint of Abdo Kids
abdobooks.com

Abdo
SENSES SCAVENGER HUNT
Kids

abdobooks.com

Published by Abdo Kids, a division of ABDO, P.O. Box 398166, Minneapolis, Minnesota 55439.
Copyright © 2023 by Abdo Consulting Group, Inc. International copyrights reserved in all countries.
No part of this book may be reproduced in any form without written permission from the publisher.
Abdo Kids Junior™ is a trademark and logo of Abdo Kids.

Printed in the United States of America, North Mankato, Minnesota.

052022

092022

THIS BOOK CONTAINS
RECYCLED MATERIALS

Photo Credits: Shutterstock

Production Contributors: Teddy Borth, Jennie Forsberg, Grace Hansen

Design Contributors: Candice Keimig, Pakou Moua

Library of Congress Control Number: 2021950710

Publisher's Cataloging-in-Publication Data

Names: Davis, Bela, author.

Title: My home scavenger hunt / by Bela Davis.

Description: Minneapolis, Minnesota : Abdo Kids, 2023 | Series: Senses scavenger hunt | Includes online
    resources and index.

Identifiers: ISBN 9781098261535 (lib. bdg.) | ISBN 9781644948347 (pbk.) | ISBN 9781098262372
    (ebook) | ISBN 9781098262792 (Read-to-Me ebook)

Subjects: LCSH: Senses and sensation--Juvenile literature. | Home--Juvenile literature. | Scavenger hunting-
    -Juvenile literature.

Classification: DDC 612.8--dc23

Table of Contents

Home Scavenger Hunt

Let's go on a hunt! Can we find these things in a home?

1 red thing
----

2 spiky thing
----

3 animal sound
----

4 clean smell
----

5 sweet taste
----

6 soft thing

We have five **senses**. They can help find things.

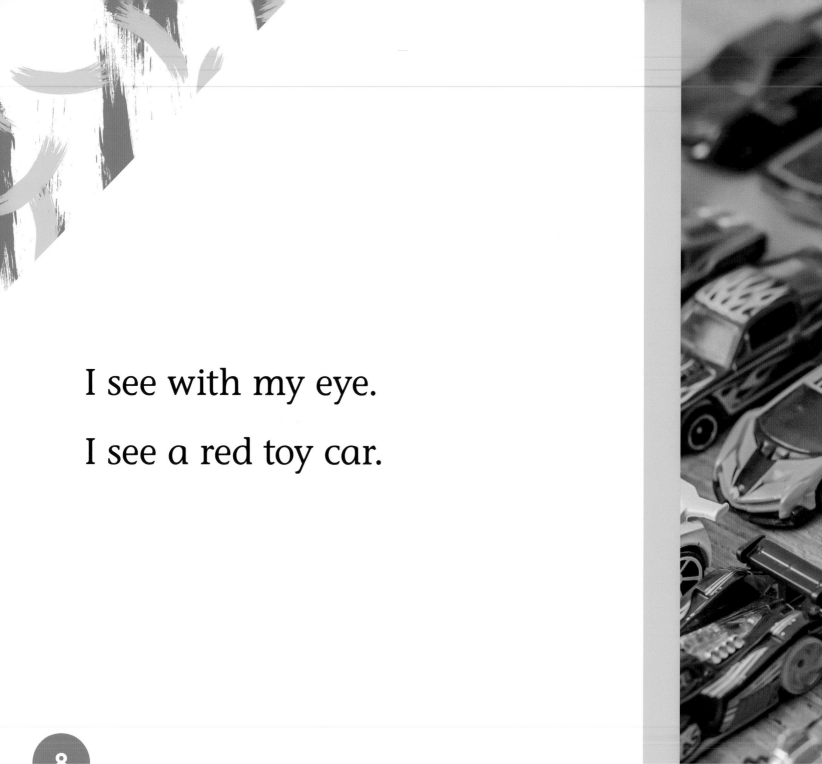

I see with my eye.

I see a red toy car.

I feel with my hand.

I feel a **spiky** plant.

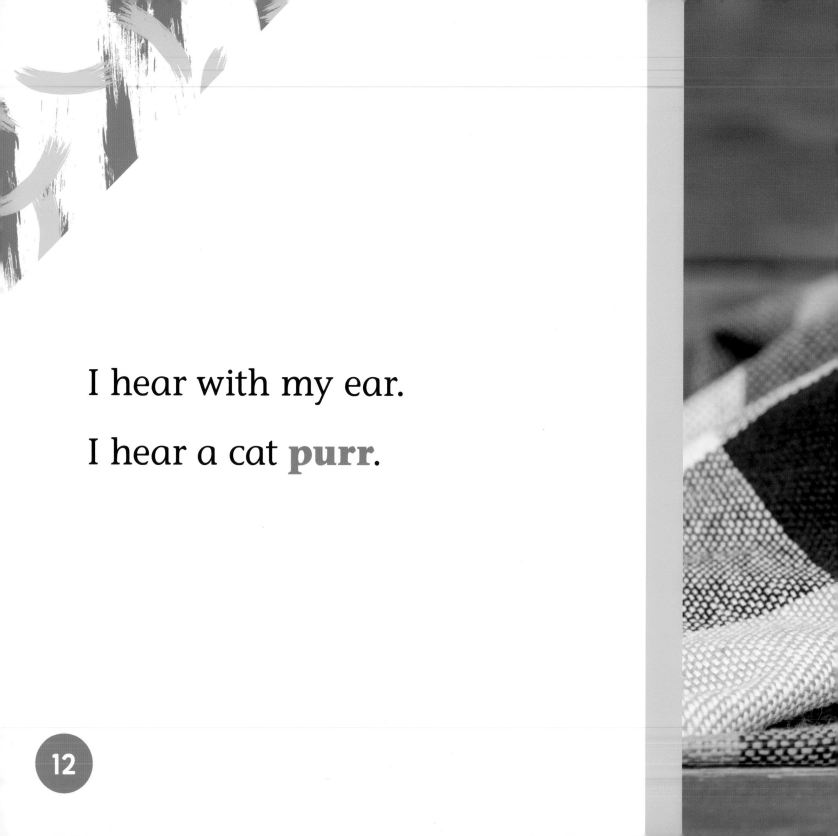

I hear with my ear.

I hear a cat **purr**.

I smell with my nose.

I smell a clean towel.

I taste with my tongue.

I taste a sweet apple.

I feel with my foot.

I feel a soft ball.

We found all 6 things!
Can you find them in your
home? Happy hunting!

Make Your Own Scavenger Hunt

Decide Where to Go

Make a List of Things You May Find

Add Senses to That List

Find Your Things!

Glossary

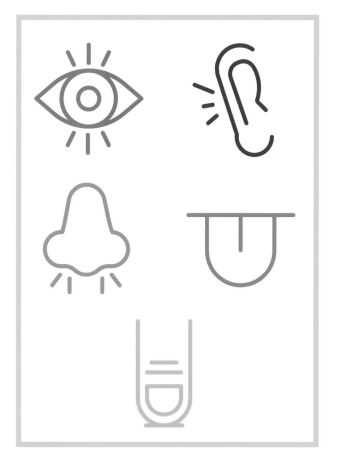

purr
a soft, low, rumbling sound made by a happy cat.

spiky
long and sharp-pointed.

sense
any of five ways to experience one's surroundings. The senses are sight, hearing, smell, taste, and touch.

Index

Abdo Kids
ONLINE
FREE! ONLINE MULTIMEDIA RESOURCES

Visit **abdokids.com** to access crafts, games, videos, and more!

Use Abdo Kids code
SMK1535
or scan this QR code!